THE ELEMENTS

Mercury

Susan Watt

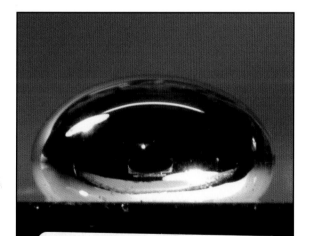

BENCHMARK BOOKS

MARSHALL CAVENDISH

NEW YORK

Benchmark Books
Marshall Cavendish
99 White Plains Road
Tarrytown, New York 10591

www.marshallcavendish.com

Library of Congress Cataloging-in-Publication Data

Watt, Susan, date.
Mercury / by Susan Watt.
p.   cm. — (The elements)
Includes index.

ISBN 0-7614-1814-8
1. Mercury—Juvenile literature. I. Title. II.
Elements (Benchmark Books)
QD181.H6W38 2005
546'.633—dc22

2004047633

Printed in China

Picture credits
Front Cover: Image State
Back Cover: Topham Picturepoint: The British Library/HIP

2004 RGB Research Ltd: www.element-collection.com 30
Corbis: Jose Manuel Sanchis Calvete 7t, Jose Luis Pelaez Inc 17, Charles Philip 25b,
Sakamoto Photo Research Laboratory 7b, Michael S Yamashita 26
G Donald Bain: The Geo-Images Project/University of California, Berkeley 14t, 14b
Image State: 4
Imagingbody.com: 27
Mary Evans Picture Library: 10
National Laboratory of Medicine: 11, 22
Pacific Northwest National Laboratory: 25t
Photos.com: 6, 23
Science Photo Library: Sinclair Stammers 21, Charles D Winters 3, 13 16
Science & Society Picture Library: Science Museum 8, 24
Topham Picturepoint: 1, 12, John Maier Jr / The Image Works 18, The British Library/HIP 19

Series created by The Brown Reference Group plc.
Designed by Sarah Williams
www.brownreference.com

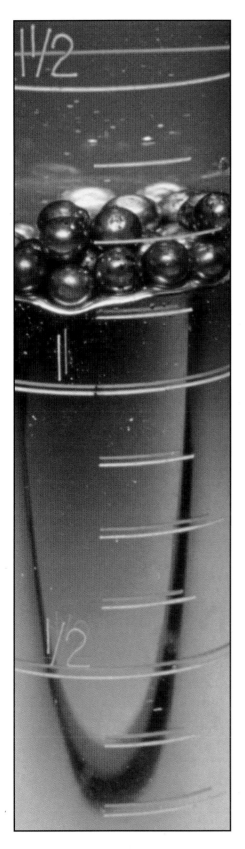

Contents

What is mercury?

Isotope	Proportion in nature
Hg-196	0.15%
Hg-198	9.97%
Hg-199	16.87%
Hg-200	23.10%
Hg-201	13.18%
Hg-202	29.86%
Hg-204	6.87%

Mercury is one of the most unusual elements because it is a metal that is liquid at room temperature. This is unique among metals. Mercury is a very nice-looking element, but it is also highly poisonous. Despite this, mercury has been used from ancient times for many things, including refining gold and filling teeth.

Mercury atoms

Like all elements, mercury is made up of atoms. Atoms are tiny particles that make up an element. The structure of an atom defines how it behaves. Atoms contain even smaller particles: protons, neutrons, and electrons. Neutrons and protons have about the same mass. Electrons are much lighter than protons or neutrons. All mercury atoms have 80 protons in their nucleus (center), and 80 electrons orbiting around that nucleus.

Mercury is a liquid at room temperature because its atoms are too small to bond together strongly.

The number of neutrons in each atom varies. Some mercury atoms have as many as 124 neutrons in the nucleus, while others have just 116. Atoms with different numbers of neutrons are called isotopes. Mercury has seven natural isotopes.

Liquid metal

Electrons are negatively-charged, and they are attracted to the positively-charged protons in the nucleus. Neutrons are not charged. The electrons in atoms are arranged in shells. Each shell holds a certain number of electrons. The electrons in the outer shell are involved in reactions with other atoms and are used for forming bonds. Mercury has two electrons in its outer shell. It forms compounds with other atoms by donating or sharing these two electrons.

In most metals, the outer electrons are not held strongly by each nucleus. Instead they form a pool of electrons that is shared by all the atoms. This bonds the atoms together and gives metals their strength.

Mercury atoms, however, are smaller than atoms of elements with a similar mass. As a result, the electrons are held tightly by the nucleus, and only a few electrons join the pool of electrons. This holds the mercury atoms together only weakly. The weak bonds give mercury a low melting point, so it is a liquid at room temperature.

MERCURY ATOM

Nucleus

Sixth shell

Fifth shell

Fourth shell

Third shell

Second shell

First shell

The number of positively charged protons in the nucleus of any atom is balanced by the number of negatively charged electrons outside it. Mercury atoms have 80 protons and 80 electrons. The electrons orbit the atom in 6 shells. There are 2 electrons in the first shell, 8 in the second, 18 in the third, 32 in the fourth, 18 in the fifth, and 2 in the sixth and outermost shell.

Mercury in nature

Hot lava from volcanoes sometimes heats minerals containing mercury, releasing pure mercury.

Mercury exists in rocks, but it is present in only tiny amounts. There are 3.5 ounces (100 g) of mercury in every 1,000 tons (900 tonnes) of rock. In some rocks the proportion of mercury is much higher. For example, shale is a rock made of clay. Out of every five million atoms in the shale, two of them are mercury atoms. This is more mercury than in most substances. Sandstone has three mercury atoms in every 100 million. Sea water has just five atoms out of 100 billion.

Mercury minerals

Mercury is as rare as silver. However, it is not considered a precious metal, like silver or gold, because there are several large and concentrated mercury sources. Mercury is generally found in nature combined with other substances making mineral compounds. It is still a high-priced metal but much less expensive than gold

---

DID YOU KNOW?

MERCURY PLANTS

You may have heard of a plant called dog's mercury (*Mercurialis perennis*) and wondered if it contains the element mercury. It does not. The name simply refers to the fact that the plant is poisonous. However, other mercury-named plants, such as herb mercury (*Mercurialis annua*), are not poisonous at all. Herb mercury is sometimes used in cooking in place of spinach.

---

or platinum. This is because mercury is easy to extract from most of its naturally occurring compounds.

The most abundant mercury-containing mineral is cinnabar, which is mercury sulfide (HgS). This bright red substance has been known as a source of mercury since ancient times. Other

These red and pink crystals are cinnabar, a common mercury-containing mineral.

naturally occurring mercury minerals include calomel, which is mercurous chloride (Hg_2Cl_2).

Pure mercury metal sometimes occurs in droplets or in larger amounts near active volcanoes or hot springs. This is because heating the mercury minerals releases mercury vapor, which then condenses into liquid metal.

DID YOU KNOW?

CINNABAR, THE ARTISTS' RED

The striking color of the mineral cinnabar has been used by artists for thousands of years. Cinnabar was widely used as a pigment in China since before 2000 B.C.E. It is also known by the name "Chinese red."

The natural color of cinnabar varies from bright reddish orange to a darker purplish red. In traditional oil paintings it was often blended with white lead paint to produce realistic-looking flesh colors. A bright red pigment called vermilion was made using mercury sulfide, the same compound found in natural cinnabar. Today, however, these pigments are seldom used because they are poisonous and do not last as long as modern paints and dyes.

This pot was made 2,000 years ago in Japan. Its red color comes from cinnabar, a mineral containing mercury sulfide.

Mercury in history

People have known about mercury since ancient times, across many different civilizations from China to Rome. It has been found in Egyptian tombs dating from 1500 B.C.E. and may have been known to Chinese civilizations even earlier. By the first century C.E. there was a brisk international trade in mercury.

Increasing supply

The Romans mined mercury but were also aware of its hazards. Only slaves were used for mining. This is because once they started working, Roman mercury miners could expect to die within six months.

Burning glasses were used to heat mercury. The lenses focus the Sun's heat onto the mercury.

DID YOU KNOW?

Hg FOR MERCURY

The element mercury used to be known as quicksilver. This is because the liquid droplets do not wet surfaces as water does, but instead run around in such a lively way that it can seem as though the metal is almost alive. The word *quick* means "alive" in old English. Mercury is still known as *Quecksilber* in German.

But neither the name mercury nor quicksilver contains the letters *H* and *g*, so why is the modern chemical symbol for mercury Hg? The Latin word for mercury is *hydrargyrum*. This means "water silver." The symbol Hg is taken from this older word.

During the Middle Ages (400–1500 C.E.), only a small amount of mercury was produced because there was little use for it. However, by the sixteenth century, mercury was in greater demand. It was used in medicine and for extracting gold and silver from rocks. When large supplies of gold were found by Spanish explorers in South America, a great deal of mercury was needed. Spanish ships would carry mercury to Mexico and then return filled with the extracted gold.

Discovering oxygen

In later years, the chemistry of mercury played a vital part in the discovery of oxygen. This then laid the foundations for the understanding of the other elements.

In 1774 the English chemist Joseph Priestley (1733–1804) noticed that when a red substance was heated, liquid mercury was formed together with an unknown gas. The red substance turned out to be mercury oxide (HgO).

A candle burned more brightly in the gas. Because a flame was thought to go out when the air contained a substance called phlogiston, Priestley called the gas dephlogisticated air.

Priestley told French chemist Antoine Lavoisier (1743–1794) of his findings. Lavoisier did the experiment the other way around. He heated mercury in a flask of air. A red substance was formed and the air left inside the flask put out flames. According to Priestley's theory, phlogiston should have been released by this reaction. However, Lavoisier found that the red substance was heavier than the mercury. This meant that mercury had combined with something else and could not have released phlogiston. Lavoisier realized that mercury was combining with a gas in the air to form the red substance. So when the red substance was itself heated, as Priestley had done, this same gas was released. Lavoisier called the gas oxygen.

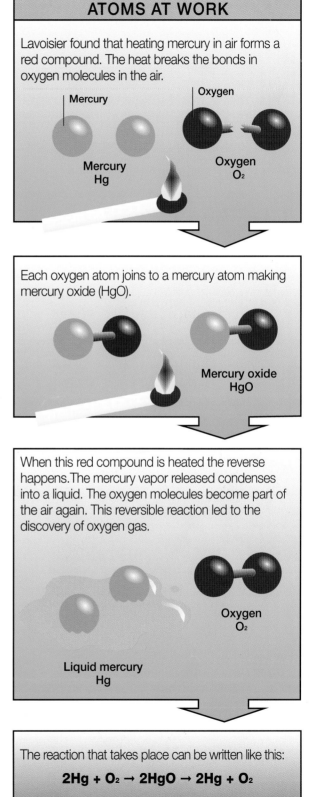

ATOMS AT WORK

Lavoisier found that heating mercury in air forms a red compound. The heat breaks the bonds in oxygen molecules in the air.

Mercury

Oxygen

Mercury
Hg

Oxygen
O_2

Each oxygen atom joins to a mercury atom making mercury oxide (HgO).

Mercury oxide
HgO

When this red compound is heated the reverse happens. The mercury vapor released condenses into a liquid. The oxygen molecules become part of the air again. This reversible reaction led to the discovery of oxygen gas.

Oxygen
O_2

Liquid mercury
Hg

The reaction that takes place can be written like this:
$$2Hg + O_2 \rightarrow 2HgO \rightarrow 2Hg + O_2$$

Mercury in mythology

Mercury is such an unusual metal that it has a unique place in myths and legends. The name *mercury* itself comes from Roman mythology, which included the god Mercurius, now called Mercury.

Moving fast

In early Roman times the god Mercury was associated with business and trade. By about 500 B.C.E., however, Mercury had been linked to the Greek god Hermes because they shared many characteristics. Hermes was the winged messenger for Zeus, the king of the gods. Mercury also became associated with speed and travel, but he did not lose his links with trade. The word *mercantile*, which means business-related, refers to this aspect of Mercury's activities. The word *mercurial*, however, describes an unpredictable person. This probably refers to the god's speed and erratic nature, also like the metal's behavior.

An eighteenth-century engraving of Mercury shows his winged shoes and cap. The staff in his left hand put anyone it touched to sleep.

Alchemists were the first chemists. They believed that all metals contained a certain amount of mercury.

The planet Mercury is named for the god. Roman astronomers noticed that this planet moved more rapidly across the sky than any other. The name Mercury, therefore, was the natural choice.

Alchemy

Early chemists were called alchemists. Although they discovered many useful chemical principles and learned a lot about common substances, alchemist were not scientists as we know them today. They often believed in magic.

Many regarded Mercury as the god of alchemy. Alchemists were sometimes thought to be wizards or witches. They had to keep their work secret so they would not get into trouble.

Many alchemists were searching for the elixir of life that would make them live forever. Others were searching for a way to make gold. According to the alchemists, mercury was the fundamental metal. They thought all other metals were made up of a mixture of mercury and sulfur. They believed each metal had set amounts of both substances and had been heated naturally underground in different ways. Alchemists hoped to figure out ways of making gold from mercury and sulfur and become rich by making the gold. They did not succeed because mercury, sulfur, and gold are separate elements that cannot be converted into one another through chemistry.

DID YOU KNOW?

MERCURY DAY

Wednesday should actually be called Mercuryday. As the Romans conquered and lived in other countries in Europe, the Roman god Mercury became merged with some of the local gods. One of these was a German god, Wodan, and the word *Wednesday* means Wodan's day. This mercury connection is more obvious in the French word for Wednesday—Mercredi.

Special characteristics

If you have ever seen mercury, you will know it is an amazing material, with a bright, silvery shine. As well as being a liquid metal, it is very dense. Density is a measure of how heavy an object is compared to its size.

Unusual liquid

Mercury does not behave like most liquids. For example, it does not soak into a surface or spread out over it. Instead it clings together in droplets. The force keeping each droplet together is called surface tension. In a glass tube, the edge of the mercury surface curves down where it meets the glass. Most liquids will curve up the other way, wetting the inside of the glass. Mercury behaves this way because the surface tension holding its atoms together is larger than in other liquids.

A droplet of liquid mercury sits on a solid surface. Mercury has a very strong surface tension which stops the droplet from spreading out.

MERCURY FACTS	
● Chemical symbol	Hg
● Atomic number	80
● Melting point	−37.8 °F (−38.8 °C)
● Boiling point	674 °F (356.7 °C)
● Density	13.6 grams in every cubic cm (13.6 times denser than water)

Physical properties

Mercury has a very low boiling point for a metal. This means that even at room temperature, mercury atoms evaporate and form vapor. This makes the metal very dangerous to handle, because mercury vapor is poisonous if breathed in.

Mercury was once used in thermometers. This uses two of mercury's most useful properties. It stays as a liquid over a wide temperature range, and it expands evenly as temperature goes up.

Mercury does conduct heat and electricity, but not well. The metal is used as a standard for electrical resistance. Resistance is the measure of how much an object resists a current flowing through it. The unit of resistance, the Ohm, is defined as the resistance of a column of mercury 41.85 inches (106.3 cm) long and with an area of 0.0015 square inches (1 square mm).

Mercury also forms amalgams. This is a mixture of other metals dissolved in liquid mercury. Mercury amalgams have been used in refining gold and silver and also in dentistry, where a type of amalgam is used for filling teeth. One of the few metals that does not form an amalgam with mercury is iron. Iron bottles are often used for storing and transporting mercury.

Mercury is a very dense element. Since copper is less dense, these balls are floating on the surface of the mercury. Water also floats on top of the mercury.

Mining and refining

Mercury-containing rocks are found all over the world. Large mercury deposits exist in the United States, Canada, Peru, Brazil, Mexico, Spain, Italy, Slovenia, Russia, China, and Japan.

Risky business

Mercury has many uses in industry, and there is plenty of mercury left to be mined. But mercury production is decreasing every year because of concerns about its poisonous nature. Several countries still produce mercury, but the last U.S. mercury mine closed in 1990.

The oldest and largest mercury mine in the world is in Spain at Almadén. It is about 140 miles (2.2 km) southwest of Madrid. This mine started producing

The most common source of mercury is the red mineral cinnabar. Mercury can be extracted from this mineral by heating it.

California once had mercury mines, such as this one at Idria. Most mercury now comes from Spain.

mercury around 400 B.C.E., and has produced about 280,000 tons (250,000 tonnes) of mercury since then. About one-third of all pure mercury has come from this single mine. Although there is still a lot of mercury underground at Almadén, large amounts of mercury are also recycled there from scrap gathered from across the world.

Refining process

The main source of mercury metal is the mineral cinnabar. This contains the compound mercury sulfide (HgS). Mercury is relatively easy to extract from cinnabar ores because heating the mineral in air is all that is required. In the refining process, the ore is crushed and mixed with charcoal. This mixture is then heated in a furnace. When the temperature reaches 1076 °F (580 °C), the mercury sulfide reacts with oxygen in the air to form mercury vapor and sulfur dioxide. This reaction produces heat, which keeps the temperature inside the furnace high and keeps the reaction going. The mercury vapor is cooled by being passed though long pipes. The vapor then condenses into liquid mercury.

The purity of the mercury produced by this simple method is very high—at least 99.9 percent. The mercury is then poured into iron flasks. Each flask contains 76 pounds (34.5 kg) of mercury. The metal is traded around the world in these flasks.

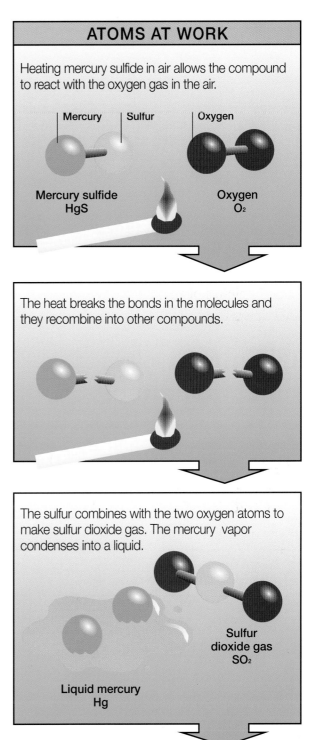

ATOMS AT WORK

Heating mercury sulfide in air allows the compound to react with the oxygen gas in the air.

Mercury | Sulfur | Oxygen

Mercury sulfide
HgS

Oxygen
O_2

The heat breaks the bonds in the molecules and they recombine into other compounds.

The sulfur combines with the two oxygen atoms to make sulfur dioxide gas. The mercury vapor condenses into a liquid.

Sulfur
dioxide gas
SO_2

Liquid mercury
Hg

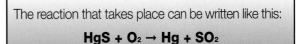

The reaction that takes place can be written like this:

$$HgS + O_2 \rightarrow Hg + SO_2$$

Chemistry and compounds

This copper mercury iodide (Cu_2HgI_4) is a heat-sensitive solid. When heated, the powder turns from red to brown. It becomes red again as it cools.

Among the elements, mercury is only mildly reactive. It forms many different compounds, but the element does not react easily with most elements.

One electron or two

Mercury atoms have two electrons in their outer shell. One or both of these can take part in reactions. When two electrons are involved, mercury (II) compounds are formed. When just one electron takes part, mercury (I), or mercurous, compounds are produced.

In mercury (II) compounds, the two mercury electrons are shared with the one or two other atoms in the compound. This sharing produces a covalent bond that locks the mercury atom to the others in the compound.

Mercury (I), or mercurous, compounds bond in a different way. Each mercury atom gives away one electron to an atom of another element in the compound. This turns the mercury atom into a positive ion. The atom that receives the electron becomes a negatively charged ion. The opposite charges of the two ions attract them to each other, forming an ionic bond.

Mercury ions often join together in pairs. The two ions use the remaining electron in their outer shells to form a covalent bond between them. A pair of mercurous ions have double the positive charge of a single ion. They have the chemical symbol Hg_2^{2+}.

Colorful chemistry

Many mercury compounds are brightly colored. For example, mercury sulfide (HgS) or cinnabar is bright red, mercurous fluoride (Hg_2F_2) and mercurous iodide (Hg_2I_2) are yellow, and mercury oxide (HgO) can be red or yellow. Mercurous chloride (Hg_2Cl_2), known as calomel, is a white solid. Strangely, its name comes from the Greek words for "beautiful black." No

Mercury fulminate is used in the detonators that set off explosives. The brown powder burns very hot and fast, making the rest of the explosive explode.

one knows quite how it got this name, although it may be because a black substance containing fine particles of mercury metal is produced when calomel is mixed with ammonia.

Many other mercury compounds have interesting properties. A complex mercury compound called Nessler's reagent is used for detecting ammonia (NH_3). If the reagent turns brown, then ammonia is present. People who keep fish use Nessler's reagent to check whether fish waste products, which contain ammonia, are dirtying the water. Dangerous mercury compounds include mercury fulminate $Hg(CNO)_2$, which is an explosive powder. Mercury chloride ($HgCl_2$) is a powerful poison. Just 0.01 ounces (0.3 g) is deadly.

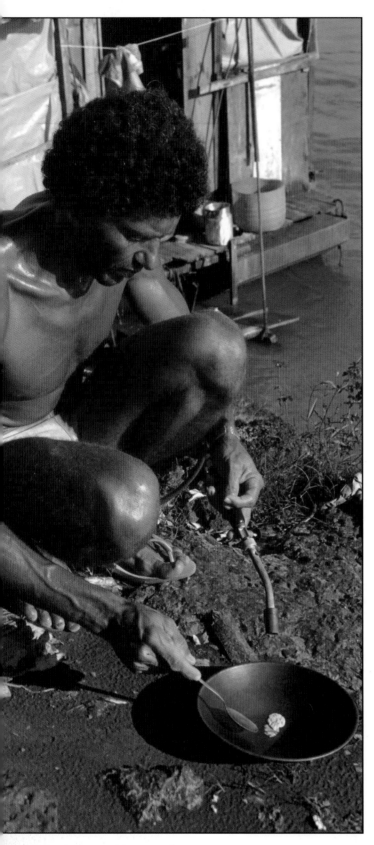

Mercury's uses

Mercury's unique properties mean that it has had many uses through the ages. But because mercury and its compounds are generally poisonous, mercury is used less frequently. In almost all its applications, from thermometers to batteries, other materials have been used instead of mercury. Even so, around 4,000 tons (3,600 tonnes) of mercury are still used each year.

Precious metals

In earlier centuries, mercury was used mainly for purifying precious metals such as gold, platinum, and silver. The impure precious metals were mixed with mercury. The atoms of the precious metal were mixed up with the mercury, forming an amalgam. The impurities did not mix with the mercury.

The amalgam was heated to boil away the mercury, leaving the pure gold or silver behind. The mercury vapor was collected and cooled back into a liquid to be used later. This purifying method is very harmful because a lot of the mercury pollutes the environment or is breathed in.

A piece of mercury-gold amalgam is heated at a gold mine in Brazil. The heat boils away the mercury leaving pure gold behind.

Splitting salt

The main use of mercury today is in making chlorine gas from salt (sodium chloride; NaCl). In this process, an electric current is passed through water containing salt. The current is passed from a carbon

The Mad Hatter (left) is a character from Alice's Adventures in Wonderland *by Lewis Carroll. In real life, many hatmakers used mercury and had mental problems due to poisoning.*

DID YOU KNOW?

MAD AS A HATTER!

The phrase "mad as a hatter" comes from the fact that hatmakers, or milliners, once really did go mad through mercury poisoning.

In the nineteenth century most men's hats were made from felt. Felt is produced by matting together fine animal fur. Beaver fur was best for this, because its fibers are rough and stick together well. Less expensive furs, such as rabbit hair, could only be used if the glossy hairs were made rougher first. This was done by brushing the fur with a solution containing mercury nitrate ($HgNO_3$). The fur was then shaved off and dipped in acid, which thickened and hardened it. The acid made the mercury nitrate become pure mercury vapor. The poor ventilation in many factories meant that workers breathed in a lot of mercury vapor. Over a long period these hatters would develop mental problems.

ATOMS AT WORK

Mercury is used to make chlorine gas from rock salt (sodium chloride; NaCl). This is done by electrolysis. Electricity is passed through a salt solution from a mercury electrode to a carbon electrode. When it dissolves, the salt crystals split into sodium and chlorine ions.

electrode to another electrode made of liquid mercury. This set up is like a giant battery. Chlorine gas is produced at the carbon electrode. Sodium atoms dissolve in the mercury electrode, forming an amalgam. Because it is liquid, the mercury–sodium amalgam is continuously pumped through the system and replaced with

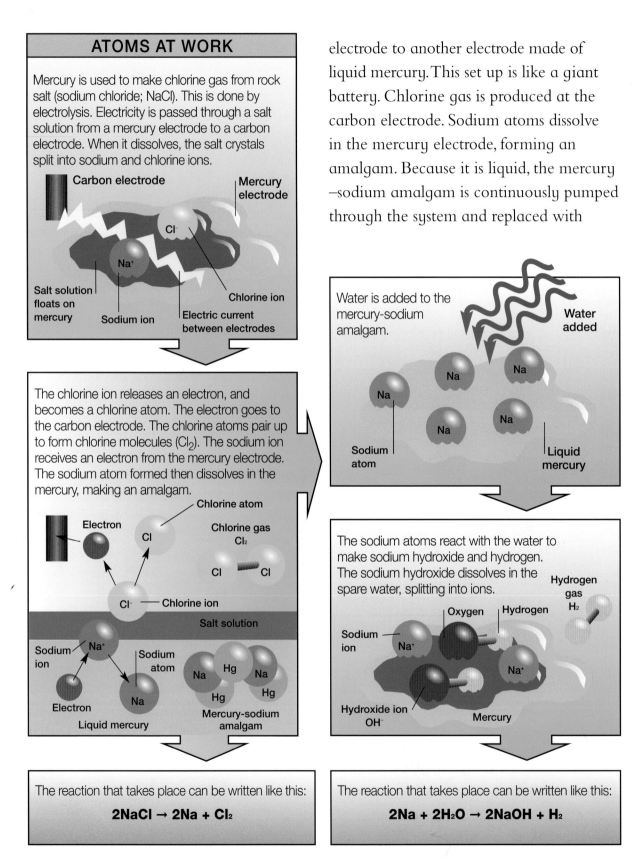

Carbon electrode

Mercury electrode

Cl⁻

Na⁺

Salt solution floats on mercury

Sodium ion

Chlorine ion

Electric current between electrodes

Water is added to the mercury-sodium amalgam.

Water added

Na

Na

Na

Na

Na

Sodium atom

Liquid mercury

The chlorine ion releases an electron, and becomes a chlorine atom. The electron goes to the carbon electrode. The chlorine atoms pair up to form chlorine molecules (Cl_2). The sodium ion receives an electron from the mercury electrode. The sodium atom formed then dissolves in the mercury, making an amalgam.

Chlorine atom

Electron

Chlorine gas Cl_2

Cl

Cl   Cl

Cl⁻ —— **Chlorine ion**

Salt solution

Sodium ion Na⁺

Sodium atom

Na   Hg   Na

Electron   Na   Hg   Hg

Liquid mercury   **Mercury-sodium amalgam**

The sodium atoms react with the water to make sodium hydroxide and hydrogen. The sodium hydroxide dissolves in the spare water, splitting into ions.

Hydrogen gas H_2

Oxygen   **Hydrogen**

Sodium ion   Na⁺

Na⁺

Hydroxide ion OH⁻

Mercury

The reaction that takes place can be written like this:
2NaCl → 2Na + Cl₂

The reaction that takes place can be written like this:
2Na + 2H₂O → 2NaOH + H₂

Safer applications

Some uses of mercury are very safe. Mercury is used in the lamps in street lights and in floodlighting. The light from these lamps has an eerie color because it is made up mainly of purple and green light. These are the colors that mercury atoms emit. Mercury lamps are also used to produce a type of light you cannot see—ultraviolet (UV) light. Tanning beds have mercury vapor lamps that produce UV light that tans people's skin.

Mercury vapor is used in fluorescent lamps, like the ultraviolet (UV) lightbulbs used above. The UV lamps are being used to light up DNA samples.

fresh mercury. The amalgam is then reacted with pure water, forming a sodium hydroxide solution and pure mercury. This mercury is pumped back into the system. Because some mercury escapes and causes pollution, this process is being stopped in most countries.

DID YOU KNOW?

FLUORESCENT TUBES

The fluorescent tubes often used in offices and shops generally contain mercury vapor. They work in a different way from normal electric lightbulbs, which have a thin piece of glowing wire. In a mercury vapor lamp, the gas inside the lamp glows.

The vapor glows when electricity flows through it. Light is produced when electrons in the electricity hit the mercury atoms in the vapor. The atoms absorb the energy in the electrons. Then they release this energy in the form of invisible ultraviolet light. A lining on the glass tube converts the ultraviolet light into visible light.

Electricity does not flow through a gas very well, so a large voltage is needed to light up the tubes. Voltage is a measurement of the force that pushes the electric current through something. Once the current is flowing, and the mercury has been heated up, a lower voltage is needed. This makes the lamps very efficient.

Measuring with mercury

U ntil the late twentieth century, mercury could be found in many homes because it was used in barometers and thermometers. Today these devices are electronic, or they use another less dangerous liquid, such as alcohol.

Measuring temperature

The mercury and glass thermometer was the first device that could measure temperature accurately. It made use of the way mercury expands as it gets hotter and contracts as it cools. The thermometers had a thin column of mercury inside them. This column changes in length according to the temperature.

The first thermometers were invented at the end of the sixteenth century. They used water instead of mercury, held in open glass tubes. These early devices were very inaccurate.

A century later, mercury was used in thermometers. These were better because mercury expands by very precise amounts with each rise in temperature. Mercury also has a higher boiling point than most liquids, so it is useful at high temperatures.

In 1714 the first accurate mercury thermometer was made by the German scientist Gabriel Fahrenheit (1686–1736),

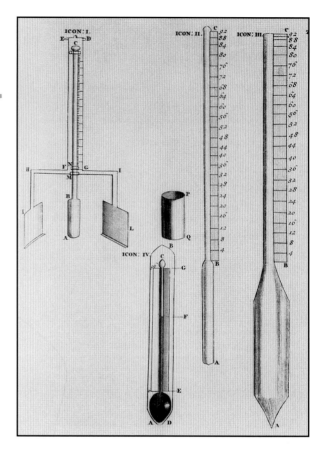

These are sketches of Gabriel Fahrenheit's early mercury thermometers. As the temperature rises, the mercury expands and moves up inside the thin glass tube. Cooler temperatures make the mercury drop.

who also developed the temperature scale still in use today. Working in Amsterdam, Fahrenheit combined the ideas of earlier instrument makers to produce his thermometers. They had a sealed glass tube containing a thin column of mercury.

Fahrenheit used the temperature of an ice and salt mixture for the lowest point on his scale and blood temperature as the upper fixed point. He divided the space in between into 90 equal intervals, or degrees.

He later changed the fixed points to the freezing point of water at 32 degrees and the boiling point of water at 212 degrees, giving today's Fahrenheit scale.

Measuring pressure

Mercury was also used in barometers. These are devices that measure the pressure of the atmosphere. Pressure is a measure of a force acting on a certain area. Air pressure is the weight of the gases in the atmosphere pushing down on things. Air pressure varies with the weather and with altitude (height).

Air pressure was discovered by the Italian scientist Evangelista Torricelli (1608–1647). He built the first barometer to prove the existence of air pressure in order to solve an important problem.

At the time scientists were puzzled why it was not possible to pump water higher than 33 feet (10 m). Torricelli realized that it was the pressure of the atmosphere that made the pumps work. This pressure did not change much and, therefore, there was a limit to the height to which water could be pumped. Since mercury is fourteen times as dense as water, atmospheric pressure could be expected to support

Mercury thermometers like these have been largely replaced with ones that use colored alcohol or electronic devices. Meteorologists still use mercury thermometers to measure air temperatures because they are more accurate than most other types.

a column of mercury only about one-fourteenth as high as a column of water. Torricelli found this to be true. He made the first barometer by filling a glass tube 35 inches (90 cm) long with mercury, and turning it upside down so that the open end was immersed in a bowl of mercury. Instead of flowing out, the mercury in the tube was held up by the pressure of the air on the mercury in the bowl. The column of mercury did not fill the tube, however. The mercury only rose to about 30 inches (76 cm) because the air pressure was slightly lower than expected. Torricelli showed that variations in pressure could be measured by changes in the height of the mercury. Most barometers are now electronic.

Torricelli's barometer experiments in 1644 proved the existence of air pressure. He demonstrated that air pressure could push down on a bath of mercury and force the liquid up inside a closed glass tube.

DISCOVERERS

INVENTING THE BAROMETER

Evangelista Torricelli (1608–1647) was an Italian physicist and mathematician who is best known for his invention of the barometer. He was educated in Rome mostly in mathematics. In 1641 he wrote a book called *Opera Geometrica*. Among many other things, this looked at the way liquids moved. Torricelli's book was read by Galileo Galilei (1564–1642) another Italian scientist. Galileo was so impressed with him that he invited Torricelli to Florence to be his assistant. Torricelli accepted the invitation, but Galileo died only months after Torricelli's arrival. Torricelli stayed on in Florence as the professor of mathematics. In 1644 he invented the barometer, which used columns of mercury to measure air pressure. The mercury rose or fell as the air pressure changed. For a time, pressure was measured in torrs. The torr unit was named for Torricelli. Torricelli also made several improvements to the design of early telescopes.

Mercury and health

Mercury and all of its compounds are poisonous. Since mercury gives off vapor so easily, it spreads through the environment quickly. Mercury, therefore, poses a health danger to everyone. These days, however, the dangers are well controlled, and fewer people become ill because of mercury poisoning.

But this was not the case in the past. People working with mercury often became ill, and suffered from shaking hands and memory loss. Chemists who used mercury often wrote about the effects of the metal on their health. This led to better standards for mercury use.

Health effects

In most cases of mercury poisoning, the metal slowly builds up in the body from breathing in the vapor or eating

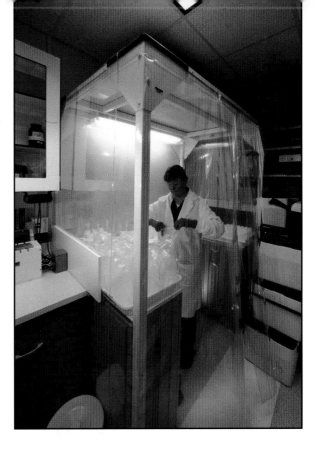

A scientist analyses the mercury content in water samples. The laboratory is kept very clean so extra mercury is not added to the samples by mistake.

contaminated food. If someone is exposed to mercury for a long time, they will develop health problems. Mercury causes damage to the lungs, kidneys, nerves, and brain. Early symptoms of mercury poisoning include numbness and tingling sensations, followed by balance and speech problems. If the poisoning continues, a person's vision and concentration are badly affected. Eventually a person will die from mercury's effects.

WARNING HEALTH HAZARD

DO NOT EAT MORE THAN ONE BASS PER WEEK, PER ADULT DUE TO HIGH MERCURY CONTENT

CHILDREN & PREGNANT WOMEN SHOULD NOT EAT BASS

Because some rivers and lakes are so polluted with mercury, eating the fish that live in them is dangerous.

DID YOU KNOW?

MERCURY AT MINAMATA

A famous incident of mercury poisoning occurred in Minamata, Japan. It began in 1953 when a child in Minamata showed signs of brain damage with no known cause. By 1956 there had been another 78 similar cases and seven people had died. It was not until 1959, however, that the cause of "Minamata disease" was discovered to be mercury. The town of Minamata was on the coast, and the residents' diet included a lot of fish. A nearby plastics factory was dumping mercury into the water, so the fish and shellfish eaten by the townspeople were filled with mercury. In all, over 3,000 people were affected by the poisoning, and about 100 people died.

An even worse case of mercury poisoning occurred in Iraq in 1971, when grain intended for sowing was used instead to make bread. The grain had been treated with a mercury compound as a preservative, so the bread was very poisonous. As a result, 6,350 people needed hospital treatment, and 459 people died.

In food

Methyl mercury is the most dangerous mercury compound because it is found in large amounts in many fish. Bacteria produce methyl mercury naturally from the mercury dissolved in seawater. It is most concentrated in large hunting fish such as swordfish and tuna. These fish eat other fish, and the mercury builds up slowly in their bodies. Shellfish, such as

The survivors of the mercury poisoning at Minamata, Japan, demonstrate against the company that caused the problem.

mussels and oysters, can also concentrate methyl mercury to a high level. They may have up to 100,000 times more mercury in them than the water in which they live. Pregnant women are advised not to eat swordfish or too much tuna. Some communities that traditionally eat a lot of fish may also be at risk.

In medicine

Another uncommon, but even more dangerous source of mercury poisoning, is from some traditional medicines. These are made from herbs and parts of animals, and

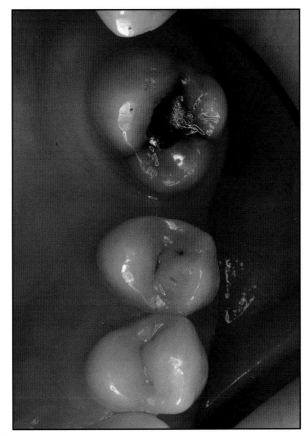

Mercury is used in some dental fillings. The metal fillings are used to fill holes caused by tooth decay.

many contain a lot of mercury. Taking these medicines in the amounts advised by the makers could mean eating nearly 0.05 ounces (1.4 g) of mercury a day.

Not all mercury compounds are so poisonous. Some have been used as successful drugs. For example, calomel (mercurous chloride, Hg_2Cl_2) was used as a diuretic. That is a substance that helps the body get rid of water. Mercury compounds have been used as disinfectants and in ointments for skin diseases.

Periodic table

Everything in the universe is made from combinations of substances called elements. Elements are made of tiny particles called atoms. These are far too small for people to see.

The character of an atom depends on how many even tinier particles called protons there are in its center, or nucleus. An element's atomic number is the same as the number of protons.

Scientists have found around 110 different elements. About 90 elements occur naturally on Earth. The rest have been made in experiments.

All these elements are set out on a chart called the periodic table. This lists all the elements in order according to their atomic number.

The elements at the left of the table are metals. Those at the right are nonmetals. Between the metals and the nonmetals are the metalloids, which sometimes act like metals and sometimes like nonmetals.

- On the left of the table are the alkali metals. These elements have just one electron in their outer shells.

- Elements get more reactive as you go down a group.

- On the right of the periodic table are the noble gases. These elements have full outer shells.

- The number of electrons orbiting the nucleus increases down each group.

- Elements in the same group have the same number of electrons in their outer shells.

- The transition metals are in the middle of the table, between Groups II and III.

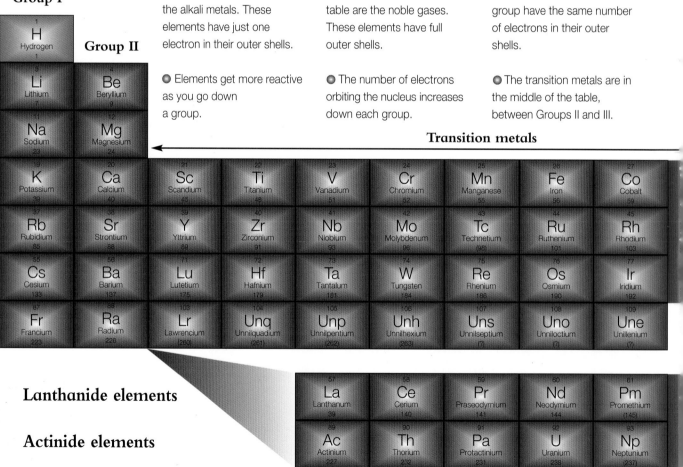

Group I

Group II

Transition metals

Lanthanide elements

Actinide elements

The horizontal rows are called periods. As you go across a period, the atomic number increases by one from each element to the next. The vertical columns are called groups. Elements get heavier as you go down a group. All the elements in a group have the same number of electrons in their outer shells. This means they react in similar ways.

The transition metals fall between Groups II and III. Their electron shells fill up in an unusual way. The lanthanide elements and the actinide elements are set apart from the main table to make it easier to read. All the lanthanide elements and the actinide elements are quite rare.

Mercury in the table

Mercury is a unique metal because it is liquid at room temperature. Only one other element, bromine in group VII, is also a liquid at room temperature. Mercury is not highly reactive but will form compounds with most nonmetals. It mixes with other metals to form amalgams. These are liquid mixtures of metals.

- Metals
- Metalloids (semimetals)
- Nonmetals

Key:
- 80 — Atomic (proton) number
- Hg — Symbol
- Mercury — Name
- 201 — Atomic mass

			Group III	Group IV	Group V	Group VI	Group VII	Group VIII
								2 He Helium 4
			5 B Boron 11	6 C Carbon 12	7 N Nitrogen 14	8 O Oxygen 16	9 F Fluorine 19	10 Ne Neon 20
			13 Al Aluminum 27	14 Si Silicon 28	15 P Phosphorus 31	16 S Sulfur 32	17 Cl Chlorine 35	18 Ar Argon 40
28 Ni Nickel 59	29 Cu Copper 64	30 Zn Zinc 65	31 Ga Gallium 70	32 Ge Germanium 73	33 As Arsenic 75	34 Se Selenium 79	35 Br Bromine 80	36 Kr Krypton 84
46 Pd Palladium 106	47 Ag Silver 108	48 Cd Cadmium 112	49 In Indium 115	50 Sn Tin 119	51 Sb Antimony 122	52 Te Tellurium 128	53 I Iodine 127	54 Xe Xenon 131
78 Pt Platinum 195	79 Au Gold 197	80 Hg Mercury 201	81 Tl Thallium 204	82 Pb Lead 207	83 Bi Bismuth (209)	84 Po Polonium (209)	85 At Astatine (210)	86 Rn Radon (222)

62 Sm Samarium 150	63 Eu Europium 152	64 Gd Gadolinium 157	65 Tb Terbium 159	66 Dy Dysprosium 163	67 Ho Holmium 165	68 Er Erbium 167	69 Tm Thulium 169	70 Yb Ytterbium 173
94 Pu Plutonium (244)	95 Am Americium (243)	96 Cm Curium (247)	97 Bk Berkelium (247)	98 Cf Californium (251)	99 Es Einsteinium (252)	100 Fm Fermium (257)	101 Md Mendelevium (258)	102 No Nobelium (259)

Chemical reactions

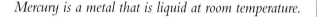

Chemical reactions are going on around us all the time. Some reactions involve just two substances; others many more. In a chemical reaction, the atoms stay the same. They join up in new combinations to form molecules.

Writing an equation

Chemical reactions can be described by writing down the combinations of atoms and molecules before and after the

Mercury is a metal that is liquid at room temperature.

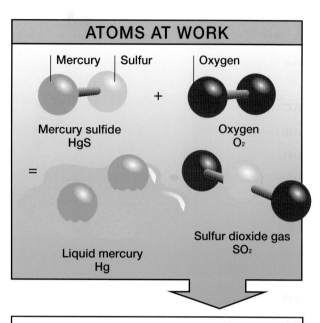

ATOMS AT WORK

Mercury · Sulfur + Oxygen

Mercury sulfide
HgS

Oxygen
O_2

=

Liquid mercury
Hg

Sulfur dioxide gas
SO_2

The reaction that takes place when mercury sulfide reacts with oxygen is written like this:

$$HgS + O_2 \rightarrow Hg + SO_2$$

This tells us that one molecule of mercury sulfide reacts with one molecule of oxygen gas to make one mercury atom and a sulfur dioxide molecule.

reaction. Since the atoms stay the same, the number of atoms before will be the same as the number of atoms after. Chemists write the reaction as an equation. This shows what happens in the chemical reaction.

Making it balance

When the numbers of each atom on both sides of the equation are equal, the equation is balanced. If the numbers are not equal, something is wrong. The chemist adjusts the number of atoms involved until the equation balances.

Glossary

acid: A chemical that releases hydrogen ions when dissolved.

atom: The smallest part of an element having all the properties of that element. Each atom is less than a millionth of an inch in diameter.

atomic number: The number of protons in an atom.

amalgam: A liquid mixture of metals, with other metals dissolved in mercury.

bond: The sharing or exchange of electrons between atoms that holds them together to form molecules.

compound: A substance made of atoms of more than one element. The atoms are held together by chemical bonds.

condense: To turn from a gas into a liquid.

crystal: A solid consisting of a repeating pattern of atoms, ions, or molecules.

dissolve: When a solid substance mixes with a liquid, or solvent, very evenly so that the solid disappears.

electrode: A material that exchanges electrons with another electrode.

electron: A tiny particle with a negative charge. Electrons are found inside atoms, where they move around the nucleus in layers called electron shells.

element: A substance that is made from only one type of atom. Mercury is one of only two elements that are liquid at room temperature.

equation: An expression using numbers and symbols to explain how a chemical reaction takes place.

ion: An atom or molecule that has lost or gained electrons. This gives it a negative or positive electrical charge.

isotopes: Atoms of an element with the same number of protons and electrons but different numbers of neutrons.

metal: An element on the left-hand side of the periodic table.

mineral: A compound or element as it is found in its natural form in Earth.

molecule: A particle that contains atoms held together by chemical bonds.

neutron: A tiny particle with no electrical charge. Neutrons are found in the nucleus of every element except hydrogen.

nucleus: The dense structure at the center of an atom. Protons and neutrons are found inside the nucleus of an atom.

periodic table: A chart of all the chemical elements laid out in order of their atomic number.

proton: A tiny particle with a positive charge. Protons are found inside the nucleus of an atom.

reaction: A process in which two or more elements or compounds combine to produce new substances.

solution: A liquid that has another substance dissolved in it.

Index

ML

1/04